ŠEVČÍK

OPUS 2 PART 3

SCHOOL OF BOWING
TECHNIQUE

SCHULE DER
BOGENTECHNIK

ÉCOLE DU MÉCANISME
DE L'ARCHET

FOR
CELLO

ARR. FEUILLARD

BOSWORTH

Heft III *	Cahier III *	Section III *
Uebungen für die Entwickelung der Biegsamkeit und Geschmeidigkeit des Handgelenkes.	Exercices pour le développement de la souplesse du poignet.	Exercises for developing suppleness of wrist.
	Seš. III *	Тетрадь III *
	Cvičení směřující k nabytí ohebnosti a obratnosti ohbí ruky.	Упражненія для развитія гибкости кисти.

№ 29.

Uebungen mit 575 Varianten auf zwei Saiten.	Exercices avec 575 variantes sur deux cordes.	Exercises with 575 Variations on two strings.
	Cvičení o 575 změnách na dvou strunách.	Упражненія съ 575 варіантами на двухъ струнахъ.

Edited and translated by H. Brett. Edited by L. R. Feuillard and A. E. Bosworth.

Varianten des vorhergehenden Beispieles.	Variantes sur l'exemple précédent.	Variations on the foregoing example.
	Obměny předešlého příkladu.	Варіанты предыдущаго примѣра.

Mit ganzem Bogen.
Tout l'archet.
Whole bow-length.

Celým smyčcem.
Цѣлымъ смычкомъ.

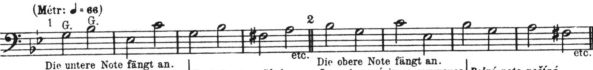

Die untere Note fängt an.		Die obere Note fängt an.	
La note inférieure commence.	*Spodní nota začíná.*	*La note supérieure commence.*	*Dolní nota počíná.*
The lower note begins.	Нижняя нота начинаетъ.	The higher note begins.	Верхняя нота начинаетъ.

Mit halbem Bogen.
Moitié de l'archet.
Half bow-length.

Polovicí smyčce.
Половиною смычка.

Mit der unteren, dann mit der oberen Hälfte.
Avec la moitié inférieure, puis avec la supérieure. *Dolejší, pak hořejší polovicí.*
First with lower, then with upper half. Нижнею, затѣмъ верхнею половиною.

4

Mit ganzem und halbem Bogen.
Tout l'archet et moitié de l'archet.
With whole and half bow-length.

Celým a polovičním smyčcem.
Цѣлымъ и половиною смычка.

Mit der Mitte.
Du milieu.
In the middle.

Středem.
Серединою

Legato.

Verschiedene Bindungen.
Différentes liaisons.
Different legati.

Různé spojky.
Различныя связи.

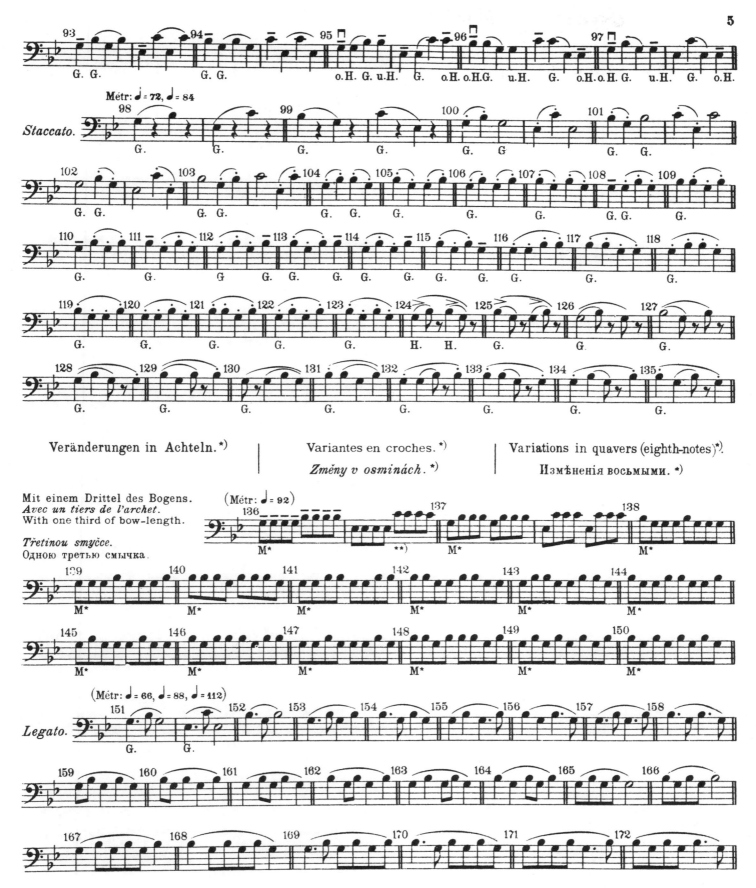

Veränderungen in Triolen.   Variantes en triolets.   Variations in Triplets.
Změny v triolách.   Измененія тріолями.

Mit wenig Bogen.
Avec peu d'archet.
With little bow.
Krátkým tahem.
Короткимъ штрихомъ.

Veränderungen in Sechzehnteln.

Variantes en doubles croches.

Variations in semiquavers (sixteenth-notes).

Změny v šestnáctinách.

Измѣненія шестнадцатыми.

Mit dem Handgelenk.
Du poignet.
With the wrist.

Ohbím.
Кистью.

Punktierte Achtel.
Croches pointées.
Dotted quavers (eighth-notes).

Tečkované osminy.
Восьмыя съ точкою.

B. & Cᵒ 6126

12

Sautillé.

Geworfenes Staccato.
Staccato jeté.
Thrown staccato.

Staccato úhozem.
Отскакивающее ст.

Springendes Staccato.
Staccato sautillant.
Hopping staccato.

Staccato skákavé.
Прыгающее стаккато.

B.& C? 6126

№ 30.

Uebungen für das Ueberspringen einer oder zweier Saiten.
Beispiel mit 190 Varianten.

Exercices pour passer une ou deux cordes.
Exemple avec 190 variantes.
Cvičení v přeskocích jedné nebo dvou strun.
Příklad se 190 proměnami.

Exercises for skipping over one or two strings.
Example with 190 Variations.
Упражненія для перескакиванія черезъ одну или двѣ струны.
Примѣръ съ 190 варіантами.

Varianten. Variantes. Variations. Варіанты.

B. & Cº 6126

Mit dem Handgelenk.
Du poignet.
With the wrist.

Ohbím ruky.
Кистью.

Staccato.

Spiccato.